Sir John
FRANKLIN

WHO WAS...

Sir John
FRANKLIN

The Man Who Ate His
Own Boots

MARTYN BEARDSLEY

Illustrations by Alex Fox

✱ SHORT BOOKS

A CIP catalogue record for this book
is available from the British Library.

Illustration copyright © Alex Fox 2005
Quiz by Sebastian Blake

ISBN 1-904977-16-2

Printed in Great Britain by
Bookmarque Ltd Croydon Surrey

"We perceived our strength decline every day…"
**Lieutenant J. Franklin, Fort Enterprise,
Northern Canada, October 1821**

Chapter One

John Franklin tried to shift his position, hoping to make himself more comfortable; but it was no good – the chafing of his feeble body against the wooden floorboards of the cabin was excruciatingly painful. His mind drifted hazily… even thinking was too much effort – although one thought stood out above all others, and hurt him far more than the pains of the cold and starvation. His death would mean that his great dream would never be achieved: the discovery of the North West Passage.

***

Back in the early 19th century, anyone who wanted to sail to the other side of the world had to undertake a long and dangerous voyage. The fruits of the journey were potentially very valuable – silks and spices from far-off countries like China and India could be sold for a lot of money in Britain and Europe – but the route was laced with hazards. You had to sail thousands of miles to the south, either by way of the Cape of Good Hope, South Africa, or the dangerous waters of Cape Horn off South America – and you ran the constant risk of storms and shortage of food and water.

For centuries, people had believed that there might be a shorter and faster way round: a passage through the icy waters off the northern coast of Canada. Many sailors had tried to get through via this route and failed, beaten by the extreme cold and frozen seas. Icebergs as big as buildings battered the wooden-hulled ships. Inlets of icy water opened up invitingly – only for the way ahead to be blocked by more ice, the sea behind freezing up once more, and trapping unwary mariners. If they were lucky, the ice would crack and creak, and they would be free again. If not they could remain hemmed in the whole winter – even worse, the pressure from the surrounding ice could slowly crush their ship to pieces.

But still the hope remained that, at least in the summer months, a clear passage could be found through the numerous islands and channels in the region: an unexplored area which on maps of the early 1800s was shown as blank spaces.

John Franklin knew that discovering the North West passage could make him lots of money, but this was not what interested him. John's heroes were brave and brilliant explorers, like Captains James Cook and his own relative Matthew Flinders – with whom he had experienced his first voyage of exploration as an eager 14-year-old midshipman. It was his greatest wish to follow in the footsteps of men like that. Now it seemed it would be left to someone else to fulfil his dream.

***

John turned his throbbing head to look at his companions. Adam, the Eskimo interpreter, lay motionless but for the laboured rising and falling of his chest. Hepburn, the loyal sailor who had stuck by John through thick and thin, stared grimly through sunken, hollow eyes at the flakes of snow blowing in through the window on a bitter Arctic wind. John wondered how his friend Dr John Richardson was coping with the weather outside. Richardson, who was around the same age as John and who had become a dear friend during their ordeals over the previous months, was the only one still strong enough among them to attempt to chop wood.

John's sad gaze moved beyond Hepburn to the far end of the room, where there rested the lifeless bodies of Peltier and Semandre, two of the Canadians helpers – known as voyageurs – hired to carry stores and equipment on the expedition. No one possessed the strength to bury them in the iron hard ground outside; they presented a stark reminder of the fate which awaited John and his remaining men.

The place in which the survivors were spending what seemed like their miserable last hours on earth was a large log cabin. They had built Fort Enterprise with their own hands as winter quarters when, full of hope and enthusiasm, the expedition had passed this way only a year ago. The deerskin parchment that had once covered the windows had been burned till brittle, and then eaten by these desperate survivors. They had done the same with their shoes, chewing each tiny morsel of leather until they were able to swallow it like some gristly piece of meat. And now there was nothing.

At least Richardson had mustered up enough energy to chop wood, so that they could feed the fire to take away some of the icy chill. But his efforts were feeble (like those of a three-year-old child), and his whole morning's work had produced just a few sticks. To make matters worse, the wood he was chopping was an outer section of the fort itself – for the trees in the surrounding forests were frozen as hard as iron – and John was worried that eventually part of the building would collapse.

It broke his heart to think of how it would pain his family and friends back in Lincolnshire to see him now: his face and torso virtually skin and bone, his limbs swollen and almost useless. A man hours from death.

He thought of Eleanor, the young poet he had hoped to marry on his return to England. They had talked just before he had set sail – yet both had been too shy to say how much they really loved each other. Now it was too late. Did she know anyway how much he cared? He could write something that might be found after his death… if only he had something to write with… if only he had the strength.

Eleanor's face grew dimmer and more distant. John felt himself drifting, his eyes closing. He wanted to sleep – but sensed it was not normal sleep that was calling him. If he gave in to it, would he ever wake again?

Then, a loud crack jolted him to his senses. His dull mind struggled to make sense of the sound: he feared the worst – had a roof or wall fallen on John Richardson? Did his friend need help? Even in his pitiful state, John prepared to make a monumental effort to somehow drag himself in the direction of the noise. And then he heard a voice. It was Richardson – giving not a cry for help, but one of excitement.

"John, look! The Indians have come – and they've brought food!"

***

One of John's young officers, the Irishman George Back, had set off weeks ago to search for the expedition's Indian helpers in the countless miles

13

of snow-shrouded forest and river around Fort Enterprise. It turned out that the Indians had believed that John would fail in his mission to explore the coastline to see if ships could pass that way. Indeed they had felt so certain he would die long before coming back to Fort Enterprise that they had not bothered to leave the promised store of food for the returning explorers.

By now, Midshipman Back had been gone for so long that John and his companions had begun to doubt whether he was even still alive; but he was, and he had finally accomplished his gruelling and dangerous mission.

The rescuers that Back brought with him from Fort Enterprise were Copper Indians, a tribe which got its name from the nearby Coppermine mountains and river. They were aghast at the sight that met their eyes. The creatures before them looked more like ghosts than men – and there were now so few of them. Out of the original team of 18 hired hands and five Britons, 11 men had lost their lives in the Arctic wilderness.

To John Franklin and his bedraggled companions, who had spent long, agonising days barely moving, with only the wind, the snow and their own gloomy thoughts for company, the speed and energy with which these fit young Indians were able to move seemed almost impossible – they were like supermen.

For more than a week, the Indians patiently nursed and fed John and his men.

"Try not to eat too quickly," Richardson warned John and the others. *"Our stomachs won't be able to cope after being empty for so long."*

Even though he was a doctor, Richardson was also only human and he was as ravenous as anyone else; like the others, he was soon wolfing the food down and later suffered from severe stomach pains, just as he had warned.

As soon as they were strong enough to walk, the Indians led the British explorers out of Fort Enterprise for the last time and took them to their own encampment, where they met up with Akaitcho. He was the Copper Indian chief who had been their guide at the start of the expedition. And it was he who had promised to leave food for John and his companions at Fort Enterprise.

Akaitcho and his people were shocked by the sight of John Franklin and his companions, and did everything they could to help. Akaitcho himself prepared a meal for them: something which, as leader of the tribe, he would never normally be expected to do, even for honoured guests. Perhaps he felt guilty about having let the explorers down.

It would take a long, long time for the survivors to fully recover from the ordeal which had so nearly pushed them to breaking point. John and Dr Richardson spent six months regaining their strength and health at a fur trading post before John was ready for the voyage home.

***

When John Franklin arrived back on English soil, he had been away for three years and had travelled over five thousand miles through some of the harshest regions on earth. This was the first expedition he had ever led. He had made mistakes and he had lost many men.

But equally the expedition had suffered more than its share of misfortune, and John had been let down by Akaitcho and others along the way. As far as the British people were concerned, John was a hero. Not only did the drama and horror of what he had been through capture the world's imagination; his achievements in charting previously unknown regions near and along the coast of North America were of great scientific value and helped pave the way for future exploration.

On his return home, John spent his time writing up an account of the voyage (a task he hated!) and spending time with loved ones. In particular, he finally plucked up the courage to propose to Eleanor.

When they got married a few months later, John Franklin was already planning a return to the Arctic.

Chapter Two

In 1800, a small, rather chubby boy, with curly brown hair, stood on the quayside. He wore white trousers, a blue checked shirt, and a blue jacket with gold anchor buttons down the front: all stiffly new and smelling of mothballs rather than sea salt. It was the uniform of a midshipman in the Royal Navy.

He was waiting to board the little boat bobbing and bumping in the waters at the foot of the stone steps below – but he wasn't looking at that small craft. He was gazing out at the fleet of majestic warships anchored out in Yarmouth Roads, and wondering which one was the *Polyphemus*. Warships were often referred to by the number of cannons they carried, and a "sixty-four" like the *Polyphemus* was a standard-sized fighting vessel.

It was not easy for John's untrained eye to pick her out from among the many line-of-battle ships, with their three tall masts and two rows of guns. Smaller boats moved busily here and there among the big wooden ships bringing supplies of all kinds, for there were rumours of a forthcoming battle – an important one – though no one seemed to know where or when.

As he took the scene in, there was excitement and even apprehension in the boy's bright eyes – but not fear, for this was his dream come true.

The boy was John Franklin, and the *Polyphemus* was to be his new home, his new life. "It was not either a youthful whim of moment, or the attractive uniforms, or the hopes of getting rid of school that drew me to it," John wrote to his mother about his decision to go to sea instead of going into business as his father had hoped. "No! I pictured to mind both the hardships and pleasures of the Sailor's life, (even to the extreme) before it was ever told to me… My mind was then so steadfastly bent on going to sea, that to settle to business would be merely impossible."

John's father had wanted him to follow in his footsteps and learn the ways of commerce in the small market town of Spilsby, Lincolnshire, where they lived. Some said it was the excitement of his first trip to the coast and sight of the sea which had made him go against his father's wishes – but it is more likely to have been the example of his relative, Matthew Flinders, who was in the process of carving out a successful career as an explorer for the Royal Navy.

Either way, John had persuaded his father to sign him up for a short spell on a merchant ship, after which, thanks probably to the Flinders connection, a place on board the *Polyphemus* had been found for him

"Take yer sea chest now, Mr Midshipman, sir?" asked a gnarled old sailor, jolting John back to reality. He was close enough to smell the chewing tobacco on the sailor's breath. The man wore a straw hat, indicating that he had recently returned from a voyage in a hot climate, and his plaited black hair reached far down his back in the traditional fashion. He had been a sailor since before John was born, yet he knew his place and spoke to the new arrival respectfully. Once on board ship, even the youngest, most junior officer like John had the power to cause any sailor who stepped out of line to be severely punished.

Despite his enthusiasm, it took John – still only 14 years old – some time to get used to this new world he had entered. Midshipmen were the lowest ranking officers. They were generally either boys like John: newcomers eager to learn and gain promotion to the rank of lieutenant; or they were older men who had never made the higher grade and never would.

In addition to learning how a ship operated, they acted as messengers between the Captain and lieutenants; they helped to maintain discipline among the men; and some, like John, helped operate the system of flags which ships used to communicate with each other.

Everything about life on board ship was different. One of the hardest things John had to accustom himself to was the system of "watches" that most men other than the Captain were obliged to follow: generally four hours awake and on duty, followed by four hours' sleep or rest, throughout the day and night. The food was not so bad while the ships were in port and able to receive fresh supplies from ashore, but once at sea things began to change. Because bread did not keep long enough, a type of biscuit was provided, often too hard to bite into, so that the sailors had to either smash it into small pieces, or soak it until soft. Like the pork and beef served to the men, the biscuit could be months or even years old before being eaten, by which time it was usually infested with maggots.

The home of the midshipman was the cockpit, down below the waterline, where no natural light could enter. It was some time before John's nose became used to the smells down here: the smell of stale air and equally stale food in the purser's stores; of the miles of old rope coated in tar; and of the slimy, stagnant water sloshing in the bilges below. The very table from which he and his companions ate their food was the one used by the surgeon to amputate smashed limbs during and after a battle.

Even the language used on board ship made John feel as though he were in a foreign country. What did it mean when they said they had to "take in the main topgallant"? How on earth did you "back the foresails and brace the main and mizzen to stop her getting in irons"?

However, there were some phrases that John recognised even though he had never before stopped to think that they had been borrowed from the sea. He was here to "learn the ropes", and now it was literally true: he would have to learn what the spider's web of rigging all around him was for. John had often described himself as being "taken aback" – but now he learned that it referred to when the wind was inadvertently allowed to blow against the wrong side of the sails and push the ship backwards. Like other children, he had sometimes been referred to as a "nipper". Now he discovered that there really were such creatures: they were the ship's boys, who used an implement that helped to "nip" and secure the ship's anchor cable as it was hauled in.

These were all things to do with the every day running of the ship; but HMS *Polyphemus* was a man-of-war, and within weeks of joining her young John Franklin was to learn the much harsher lesson of a sea battle in the age of sail. His ship was part of a large fleet sailing towards Copenhagen. The early 1800s were a time of war in Europe; Denmark had withdrawn from a treaty with Britain and declared itself a neutral country. Among other things, this meant that Britain would no longer be able to obtain from that country vital materials such as timber for masts, and it was a development the British government felt it could not afford to ignore. The Danes had refused to back down during discussions, and the British, who then had by far the most powerful navy in the world, had reluctantly decided to use force.

John was probably a signal midshipman during the Battle of Copenhagen. In the days before radio, ships communicated by hoisting flags of different colours and designs. A line of battle ships could extend for several miles, and so frigates – ships too small to take part in a fleet action – acted like mirrors, hovering some distance from the battleships and passing the Admiral's signals along the line. A signals officer like John would watch for the raising of flags through his telescope, translate the message using a codebook, write it down on a slate and pass it on to a senior officer.

***

And so to battle. As the British ships converged on the enemy, the command "Clear for Action" was given, and the sailors set about the well-rehearsed routine of transforming the ship into a sailing gun platform. Everything not needed for battle was cleared away – if time was short, some non-essential things might even be thrown over the side – the ship had to be ready to fight.

The gun ports were opened and the big guns loaded and run out. The sailors stripped to the waist and leaned out of their ports, cheering their comrades aboard the other ships into the fight. The "nippers" now became "powder monkeys", and when battle commenced they would scurry with gunpowder between the guns and the powder magazine where it was stored, located safely below the water line to reduce the chances of a cannonball or fire causing an explosion. Armed lieutenants were stationed on the gun decks to prevent any man who lost his nerve from running for safety below once the cannonballs began flying.

The *Polyphemus* was heavily engaged at

Copenhagen. She found herself taking on two ships simultaneously: one of a similar size, the other even larger. John had heard the big guns firing when the men were being trained, but this was his first time in action. The noise was deafening, the smoke blinding and choking. Massive cannonballs smashed into the ship, shredding sails, bringing rigging crashing down from above, and sending deadly splinters of wood whistling through the air. The sound of officers shouting their orders mingled with the screams of injured or dying sailors; blood washed across the decks of many vessels and ran out of the scuppers designed to let sea water drain away. It brought to John's mind a scene from hell itself.

The battle was so fierce that Admiral Hyde-Parker, commanding the fleet, ordered his ships to withdraw. It may well have been John who saw this signal and passed it on to his captain. Admiral Nelson, commanding the ships in the thick of the battle, certainly saw the signal – but, convinced that he was on the verge of victory, famously chose to ignore the order, telling his own signals officer: "You know, Foley, I have only one eye – I have a right to be blind sometimes..."

After a hard-fought battle lasting several hours, the Danes were defeated. They battered both of the enemy ships into submission, six men died and 14 were wounded in the process. John himself escaped without injury. This was by no means the last battle he would take part in – but in his heart he knew he wanted to be an explorer. As he helped with the repairs of his battle-scarred vessel, his mind was already turning towards an opportunity to pursue the dream he'd had before joining the *Polyphemus*.

Chapter Three

Even before joining the *Polyphemus*, John Franklin had hankered after a voyage of exploration. In the early 19th century, there was still much to learn about the world – in some ways expeditions by sailing ship were as fascinating to people of those times as the exploration of space is to us today.

As we have seen, a great deal of the Arctic remained uncharted; Africa was well known to Europeans but much of the interior was a mystery, and although Australia now had a small British colony there was still a great deal to discover about that vast country.

The Franklins' close ties with the family of the explorer Matthew Flinders meant that John would certainly have heard about Matthew's voyages to far-off, exotic places: in particular with the famous Captain Bligh (although Matthew was fortunately not serving on the *Bounty* when its crew mutinied). And this must have played a big part in awakening John's desire to take the unusual step of wishing to specialise in exploration rather than settle for a more routine naval career.

Prior to the Battle of Copenhagen, Matthew Flinders had been preparing an expedition to sail all the way around the coast of Australia: this was something that no one had done before – a mammoth assignment which involved making charts of every part of the coastline, recording details about the climate, the native peoples, and many other tasks.

Flinders had been scheduled to leave before John returned to England, but when John arrived home in the summer of 1801 he discovered that Flinders had been delayed – and in a last-minute rush he managed to claim a place among the hand-picked crew.

On the 18th July, 1801, HMS *Investigator* sailed from England on a voyage that would take several years to complete and, as was the case with almost all ventures of this kind, provide its fair share of hardships and perils.

***

Sailors were a superstitious lot, and although John was a devout Christian, and so perhaps less likely to believe in omens, even he might have been concerned by worrying signs at the start of the journey.

The *Investigator* was a sloop, a much smaller ship than the *Polyphemus*; she was built for speed and sailing qualities rather than battle. Nevertheless, she began leaking almost as soon as they set out, and the further they went the worse the leak became. In addition to this, before sailing, one of the crew had consulted a fortune-teller, who had said that he was going on a long voyage and that he would be shipwrecked – but not on the ship he sailed out on. Word soon got round among the men, and eventually reached the ears of John and the other officers. John himself would eventually have very good reason to remember this prophecy.

To begin with, as the ship headed for Cape Town on the coast of South Africa, where it would take on fresh food and other supplies, John spent much of his time studying navigation under Captain Flinders. Flinders was impressed by the boy's enthusiasm and intelligence, and John soon became one of the Captain's most trusted assistants.

"Without a good knowledge of navigation you'll never rise any higher in His Majesty's navy," Flinders said to him, as they sat in the shade of a tree in False Bay, near Cape Town. "You do plan to make Lieutenant, don't you John?"

"At the very least, sir!" replied John.

"Then pay close attention to all I teach you, and we shall have you there in no time!"

The *Investigator* reached Port Jackson, the landing point for the small but growing settlement of

Sydney, Australia, after a ten-month journey. After some repairs — particularly an attempt to fix the troublesome leak — and taking on more food, they set sail again to undertake their main goal of circumnavigating Australia, a task never before achieved.

Unfortunately, the ship began leaking more than ever, and many of the men had to perform the back-breaking task of pumping out water for hour after hour. Worse still, although the *Investigator*'s carpenters could not find an obvious hole where so much water could get in (the hulls of wooden ships were made of least two layers with a cavity in between, so it was not always easy to find a leak), they discovered to their alarm that a great deal of the ship's timber was rotten and in a very dangerous state. They reported to the Captain that the vessel might only last a few more months.

As for John, seven months after leaving Port Jackson, he began to feel tired and weak, and noticed sore, itchy spots had begun appearing on his arms and legs.

"Sir," he reported to Captain Flinders one morning, "may I request permission to see the ship's surgeon?"

The Captain examined John's sores and smiled grimly. "Aye, Mr Franklin – but I'm afraid there is not much he can do for you. It's the scurvy, lad. Many have the symptoms – including me."

"Is there nothing to be we can do about it, sir?" John asked.

"As soon as we can land and obtain provisions our problems will be at an end. I follow the example of the great Captain James Cook – plenty of fresh fruit and vegetables will always overcome the scurvy."

They struggled on for another month, until at last the *Investigator* was able to land at Timor off the north coast of Australia, where supplies of fresh food banished the scurvy. But it was here that they came into contact with a far more serious disease: dysentery. After many months and thousands of miles of sailing, during which Captain Flinders had carefully looked after the welfare of his crew without the loss of a single man, this severe form of diarrhoea and internal bleeding began to spread like wildfire among the men, cooped up in the cramped conditions of the small ship. By the time they made it back to Port Jackson at least nine lives had been lost.

***

After a period of rest and recovery, a new ship was obtained to carry the crew of the *Investigator*. But even now their troubles were not over.

The new ship, the *Porpoise*, was sailing through Torres Straight, off north-eastern Australia when a look-out cried frantically, *"Breakers! Breakers off the larboard bow!"* He had spotted the tell-tale white frothing waves which were every sailor's nightmare – for they were caused by the sea breaking over rocks hidden just below the surface. Everyone on the ship sprang to life: officers yelled orders and the helmsman fought with the wheel to turn the ship away. Sailors rushed to their posts ready to haul on the ropes which altered the position of the sails.

Despite their frantic efforts, there was no time. When the bottom of the ship met the jagged rocks there was a sickening grating sound accompanied by a violent juddering. Everyone was thrown to the deck. The fortune-teller's prophecy had come true.

Fortunately, on this occasion no lives were lost. But John Franklin, Matthew Flinders and nearly a hundred others found themselves stranded on a small, flat island with only the supplies they had rescued from the stricken ship to keep them alive. Flinders decided there was no alternative but for

himself and a few seamen to undertake the risky 750-mile journey back to Port Jackson in an open boat to summon help.

John and the others waited anxiously for his return. Long, empty days passed by as they gazed out to sea for the return of their Captain. Plenty of food had been rescued from the wreckage and for a while the men's spirits remained high. When six weeks had passed, though, they began to lose hope.

Then, at the beginning of October 1803, a sail was sighted on the horizon. They all rushed forward for a better view, and, before long, amid cheers from the desert island, three small ships hoved into view and anchored as close as possible to shore. Flinders had succeeded in his task, and returned for his crew – although there had been no single vessel large enough to take all the stranded men, so now the group would have to be split up.

John Franklin and Matthew Flinders were to go their very different ways. Captain Flinders boarded the *Cumberland* and headed for England, soon to be beset by more bad luck. Not long after setting out, his ship developed problems and he was forced to put in at the island of Mauritius for repairs. Unbeknown to him, a brief peace between Britain and France had come to an abrupt end while he had been at sea, and the island was now held by the French. Although Flinders produced his special "passport" – a document produced by agreement between Britain and France to protect explorers from capture in order that they might continue to carry out their valuable work – he was arrested as a spy and kept on the island for seven frustrating years, during which time a long-standing health problem grew worse. He would die just a few years after returning to England, still a comparatively young man.

John was put on to a ship bound for China so that he could to get a passage home on one of the regular trading ships – but his adventures were not over either. He found himself leaving China on board the *Earl Camden*, one of a group of 16 merchant ships transporting cargoes of tea back to England. He was weary, having endured illness, fatigue and the loss of most of his possessions when the *Porpoise* was wrecked.

But there was no time to relax. It was known that there was a squadron of French warships in the vicinity, and so John and the rest of the Royal Navy men were divided between three of the biggest ships, where they set about doing all they could to disguise them as warships, albeit small ones, escorting the convoy.

All merchant sailors dreaded being press-ganged into the Royal Navy, which meant they might have to spend years away from home, and risk their lives in battle. But in this case the merchant sailors couldn't help being impressed by the disciplined but cheerful Navy men as they responded sharply to each command and scampered around their new ships, doing their best to make the vessels look more powerful than they really were.

Sure enough, the British ships were soon spotted by the French squadron. At least five sails appeared on the horizon, and headed ominously towards them. Although thy were more numerous, the merchantmen had nothing like the firepower of the enemy.

The lead French ship was the *Marengo* – at 84 guns far mightier even than John's old *Polyphemus*. Alone it could easily wreak havoc among the trading ships, and here it was escorted by two heavy frigates and two smaller armed vessels. A merchant fleet in such circumstances would normally either try to outrun the warships, or surrender.

In spite of this, Commodore Dance, in charge of the merchant fleet, emboldened by his battle-hardened Royal Navy men and the modifications they had made to his ships, decided to bluff the French.

"Mr Franklin," said Commodore Dance as he stood on the quarterdeck of the Earl Camden with his telescope trained on the French ships.

John stepped forward. "Yes, sir?"

"I believe you are familiar with the code of signalling employed on board a man o' war?"

"That's correct sir – I was on the Polyphemus at Copenhagen."

"Then you are my signals officer, sir. Send to

all ships: 'FORM LINE-OF-BATTLE'."

"Aye, sir!" cried John, trying to hide his amazement. He heard the traditional cheer go round the merchant fleet as the signal was acknowledged from ship to ship.

Amazingly, the French were so convinced by the expert battle manoeuvres and the disguises of the British fleet that they backed off for the rest of the day. The next morning when the French began to close in again, Dance turned to meet them. There was a brief exchange of fire, after which the French lost their nerve and turned away – Dance even had the cheek to chase them for several miles! The newspapers back in England were soon as full of praise for this episode. It was as if a major battle had been won!

John's heart lifted when his ship entered the English Channel in August 1804 and he sighted Beachey Head. He began a letter to his father immediately so that it would be ready to send as soon as they landed. He had experienced a voyage, he wrote, "which has been attended with many fatigues, but more pleasures… dampened by the imprisonment of Captain Flinders at Mauritius". He was finally home after three years at sea and a journey to the other side of the world.

***

There would be further voyages of exploration ahead for John Franklin in the future, but first his country needed him for one last battle. It was to be the most important naval engagement in his country's history: the Battle of Trafalgar.

In October 1805, just over a year after his Australian adventure, 19-year-old Signal Midshipman Franklin stood on the poop deck (at the stern) of the famous 74-gun *Bellerophon*. The ship was bearing down on the combined French and Spanish fleets off Cape Trafalgar, southern Spain, and thus joined one of the bloodiest battles ever witnessed between fleets of sailing ships. The *Bellerophon* always seemed to be in the thick of any action and was known to some as the "bravest of the brave".

To the ordinary sailors, not impressed by strange sounding foreign words, she was the *Billy Ruffian*.

It was a bright, clear morning, and looking down at the quarterdeck John could see the sun glinting off the gold braid of his Captain's uniform. The First Lieutenant was trying, without success, to persuade Captain Cooke to change into a plain uniform so that he would make a less obvious target. The same scene was being enacted on board the *Victory,* where Admiral Nelson was leading the attack – and neither men would live to see the end of the encounter.

The gun crews chalked *"Bellerophon – Death or Glory!"* on their massive black cannon as they closed in. This was to be a close range fight, and the *Bellerophon* actually crashed into her first opponent, *L'Aigle (The Eagle)* so that they became entangled. They continued firing into each other at such close range that men from both sides could reach out of the gun ports and grab at each other's ramrods – the implements used for loading the guns.

After a time, John saw through the smoke of war

that, although the ship was being fired at by several of the enemy, most of the damage was still being done by *L'Aigle*, which had men in the rigging shooting and throwing hand-grenades down at him and his colleagues. Within less than 20 minutes, only eight out of 58 men were left standing on *Bellerophon's* upper decks; masts, sails and rigging had come crashing down; and the rudder, which controlled the ship's direction, was destroyed. Fires broke out several times, but brave sailors quickly scrambled to extinguish them before they got out of hand.

At the height of the battle, both the *Bellerophon's* Captain and a man standing next to John were shot dead by a sniper stationed high up in *L'Aigle's* rigging, and John himself had to dodge behind the mast when the man began to target him.

Down below in *L'Aigle* the damage wreaked by the *Bellerophon's* guns was beginning to take effect. British sailors were famous for being able to fire their guns faster and aim more accurately than any of their enemies. For some time they had been firing straight into the side of the other ship, causing such damage and destruction among the guns that eventually their opponents stopped firing back.

The *Bellerophon*'s cannon could now be directed upwards at the French seamen who were gathered on the deck, trying to clamber across to take the ship by hand-to-hand fighting. The cannon could also be directed towards the French snipers, positioned high up in the masts and rigging, who had killed many men on the upper decks of the *Bellerophon* with their musket fire and hand grenades.

This proved to be the decisive act, and eventually *L'Aigle* could take no more. Her flag was hauled down to signify surrender. One by one John saw the surrounding ships surrender or drift helplessly away, too damaged to continue.

The *Bellerophon* was crippled but victorious, and, although the battle had tragically led to the death of Admiral Nelson, the British fleet had annihilated their enemy, and averted the threat of invasion by Napoleon's all-conquering army. In view of the carnage happening around him, it was remarkable that John escaped without a scratch – though he was left partially deaf for the rest of his life by the noise from the great guns.

Chapter Four

In 1815 the Battle of Waterloo took place, and finally brought about the defeat of Napoleon Bonaparte. He had been a brilliant but ruthless emperor of France. His armies terrorised much of Europe and threatened to invade Britain. There was peace at last, but this meant the Royal Navy was now far bigger than it needed to be, and many officers like John were left ashore on half pay – some would never to return to sea.

Fortunately, the name John Franklin had been noted by important people during the journey with Matthew Flinders. And so, when a voyage to the North Pole was planned, John was chosen to go –

and not just as another officer. Having been pro-moted to lieutenant, Franklin now had sufficient rank to command a small ship. He was given the *Trent,* and answered to the orders of Captain Buchan on the much larger *Dorothea.*

It might seem strange to talk of a sailing expedi-tion to the North Pole, since we now know that it is located in a region of solid ice. But at that time no one was exactly sure what was there, and some still believed that gaps in the ice could open up during summer months – leading to another, as yet undis-covered sea.

Needless to say, neither John's little *Trent* nor Captain Buchan's *Dorothea* made much headway once they reached the frozen seas surrounding the North Pole. They probed bravely, putting them-selves and their ships in great danger. Gaps in the ice did open up from time to time, only to close up again around them, trapping the ships and squeezing them almost to breaking point. On one occasion the *Trent* was forced more than a metre upwards by the pressure of the ice.

Both ships returned home badly damaged, but again John was commended for his handling of both the ship and its men. He was developing into a commander who was both liked and respected by those who served under him.

***

In London a young poet called Eleanor Anne Porden wrote a poem about John's expedition, which somehow came to his attention. He was so impressed by this tribute that he arranged to meet her. Not long afterwards a friend of Eleanor's, who had seen them together, said that she, "…saw at once how their acquaintance was likely to end".

Very soon John and Eleanor were in love; and over the ensuing months they spent a great deal of time together – though they were soon to be parted by another expedition, which would take John away for several years.

This was John's expedition in search of the North-West Passage – the one on which he would come within hours of starving to death and survive by eating, among other things, the soft leather shoes made by natives of the Arctic region known as moccasins.

Such were his feelings for Eleanor that he began to wonder whether the time had come to propose marriage. They met a few days before he was due to sail, and John's mind was in a whirl: would it be fair to tell her how he felt just before he was to leave for such a lengthy and dangerous mission? The trouble was that John was very shy, and struggled to pluck up the courage to talk to her about his feelings. To make matters worse, Eleanor was also much less brave about expressing herself when she and John were face-to-face.

The couple met in London shortly before John was due to set sail. In his own shy, clumsy way he tried, as they strolled and talked in the spring sunshine, to drop hints about his feelings for her, hoping that this might help her to begin to open her heart to him. It did not work. She would later write that she had not been able to feel sure of his love for her, but admitted, *"I believe you carried a large share of my heart with you, for you were certainly in my head more than I could account for…"* It seems that her shyness was every bit as painful as his, and at that moment she could not bring herself to tell him.

The result was that when they parted, neither would fully realise just how much each was on the other's mind. They could only wait and hope.

***

The quest to find the North West Passage was a huge operation, involving two main expeditions – one approaching from the east, the other from the west. The expedition from the east was a marine voyage, charged with discovering whether a path could be plotted between the north coast of Canada and the numerous islands and ice floes which had confounded sailors for centuries. Ships were being sent to probe through the Baffin Bay: a sea which separates Greenland from the north-eastern extremity of Canada. And from this sea they would

51

progress into the Lancaster Sound – a stretch of water which would be the eastern entrance to the Passage (if it existed).

John's orders were very different: this time he would not be commanding a ship at all, but an overland expedition. The plan was for him to lead a team across Canada to the Coppermine River, follow it to the sea, and explore by canoe parts of the coastline. As this was an area unknown to Europeans, Franklin needed to assess whether sailing ships could pass that way.

The whole journey of over five thousand miles would have to be undertaken on foot and by canoe, and would take them into regions where no white man had ventured before, and where food would be hard to find. Canadian voyageurs, who normally worked in the fur trade, were hired to do most of the carrying and canoeing; local Indians and Eskimos were enlisted to hunt food and act as guides and interpreters. There was no possibility of a rescue party if things went wrong. And almost everything would go wrong.

***

The journey to the coast was tough, but bearable. It was after they had arrived at the coast that things went downhill. Their small canoes did not stand up well to being tossed about in the icy sea, food was now in short supply, and the voyageurs were becoming rebellious. The Indians hired to hunt for them had let them down, and as if that weren't enough one of the worst winters in living memory was coming upon them; the animals they had hoped to hunt, such as deer and bears, were even scarcer than usual.

John pushed on as far as he dared. But on the final leg of their journey, by which time they had travelled more than 650 miles, he had to admit defeat. With a heavy heart, he gave the order to head back to Fort Enterprise, the base camp where they had spent the previous winter.

Winter was outpacing them as they trudged through deep snow and battled against freezing winds. At times it was so cold that that moisture droplets from their breath would freeze and crackle in the air as soon as it left their mouths. As the snow grew deeper, food became almost impossible to find.

Hungry and miserable, all the men grew weak. If they chanced upon a rotting carcass, it was considered a feast. Mostly they survived on a type of fungus-like weed which grew in the region called *tripe de roche*. This had a horribly acid taste. It burned their mouths and gave them stomach pains, but without it they would have surely died.

At one stage Dr Richardson almost died trying to swim across a river with a rope to enable the others to pull a raft to the other side. His arms and legs became so numb from the cold that he could no longer use them to swim, and only a brave rescue bid by one of the voyageurs saved his life. When Richardson's clothes were removed, before they froze to his body, John and the rest were shocked by the sight of him: "How thin we've become!" cried one of the voyageurs in horror. They were gazing at what looked almost like a human skeleton, and knew that they had all gradually reached the same state without realising it.

As their strength and mental powers began to fail, one by one men began to drop, or wander off in a confused and dazed condition, never to be seen again.

When Midshipman Robert Hood declined so badly that he was unable to tolerate even the tripe de roche, John called a halt and discussed the worsening situation with his fellow officers.

"I fear that if we carry on like this, none of us will make it," he shouted, trying to make his voice heard about the howling Arctic wind. "I don't think Hood can go any further, and I propose that we now need to split up in order to survive."

"I will stay with Hood and make a camp," Richardson volunteered.

"I will press on to Fort Enterprise with some of the voyageurs," continued John. "There may be Indians out hunting not too far away. Mr Back, I would like you to set off with three more voyageurs to try and make contact with them, and rendezvous with me at Fort Enterprise."

Thus, having come so far together, they reluctantly parted. Dr Richardson, and a British sailor called Hepburn built a makeshift camp, where they tended to Hood. And they were soon joined by one of the voyageurs, Michel, who had been sent by Franklin to help them.

In fact, Franklin had also sent another man, Belanger, but Michel told Richardson and Hepburn that he had gone missing on the way. Richardson soon became suspicious of Michel. Although he often went off hunting alone, he rarely brought any food back – and yet he seemed stronger and fitter than the rest of them.

One day he did arrive with some meat – which

he said was wolf meat. But in the light of subsequent events they were to look back and wonder if it really had been wolf meat – and what had really become of Belanger...

Michel's behaviour grew more unpleasant and threatening by the day. One day, when Richardson and Hepburn were away from the camp, they heard Michel and the sickly Hood arguing. Some time later they heard a shot, and when they got back to the camp, Hood was dead. There was a bullet hole in the centre of his forehead. Michel claimed to know nothing about it, and at first they assumed that Hood had reached the end of his tether and killed himself. But, on examining the wound more closely, Richardson knew that Hood could not have pulled the trigger himself.

Mindful that they were very weak and less well armed than Michel, they kept their thoughts to themselves about what had really happened. Yet they were certain that Michel would not allow them to live to tell the tale, and, when he left the camp on another of his mysterious trips, they decided that they only had one course of action left open to them.

When Michel returned, Richardson approached him with a concealed pistol, and shot him dead before he could defend himself.

***

We have seen that Franklin finally made it to Fort Enterprise – only to find that the Indian hunters had broken their promise to leave them food there. Two more men died before Richardson arrived with Hepburn. George Back eventually did find the Indians, whose aid saved the lives of John and the remaining members of the expedition.

In spite of the tragic losses, and the fact that John had barely escaped with his own life after undergoing agonies that few of us can imagine, there was still much about his expedition to be celebrated. It had succeeded in charting many miles of previously unknown territory and had also added to the meagre scientific knowledge of the region. John and his team had recorded details of the climate; and mapped the area they had explored, so that others coming after them would be better prepared.

All in all, they had made a very substantial contribution to Britain's quest for the North West Passage. They had gone some way towards deciding whether ships could pass along Canada's northern coastline, and how easily food might be obtained by anyone stuck in the ice for long periods. And they had accurately sketched the scenes around them. Very few Europeans in those days knew about Eskimos or grizzly bears, or appreciated the mountainous size of the glaciers. And when all of this information finally came out, the public were fascinated.

John's book about his Arctic overland expedition, with all its drama, tragedy and scientific findings, was an immediate hit: it quickly sold out and had to be reprinted, and soon his name was known throughout Europe and America.

Chapter Five

Before long, John Franklin was already planning a return to the Arctic. He knew that a further stretch of coastline remained to be surveyed, and, armed with the experience he now had of the region and what it took to survive there, he was confident that he could go and play his part in one of the last great challenges of exploration.

He was not leaving immediately, however. And in the meantime, there was plenty of time to pick up where he had left off with Eleanor.

While John had been away, he and Eleanor had sent letters to each other regularly. Even in the remote wilderness it was possible to have mail sent from some of the fur trading posts that were dotted around.

Eleanor Anne Porden was nine years younger than John. She was pretty, very short in height, and an award-winning poet. She had a vivid imagination and had been writing little stories since she was a child. But she had never been in good health. In particular, she suffered from violent coughing fits that distressed those who witnessed them – indeed the coughing was a symptom of a much more serious illness, as she and John were to become aware.

Once John was back in England, they wrote to each other almost daily. He was staying near her London home, though for a time they were not able see each other as much as they would have liked, since John had to shut himself away to write up his account of his expedition.

Writing did not come naturally to him, a fact that Eleanor was quick to pick up on; and to tease him she sent him a little verse which included lines like:

Heigh-ho! And well-a-day!
Was ever a wight like me distrest?
What shall I write? What can I say?
Will this or that way read the best?

Then on Valentine's Day she sent him a poem in disguised handwriting that was supposed to be from a young woman called Greenstockings, whom one or two of John's men were said to have taken a liking to. Greenstockings was the daughter of an Eskimo interpreter whom John had met in the Arctic. Her father had such a high opinion of her beauty that he was reluctant to allow her be painted in case John's Great Chief (the King of England) sent for her to be his wife!

John and Eleanor were married in London in August 1823. John was by now 37 years old, a captain in the Royal Navy and on the way to becoming one of the most famous figures of the day. (He had learned of his promotion while he was in the Arctic by letter from the Admiralty: "I have reached the top of the tree!" he wrote to a friend excitedly.)

A year after their wedding, while John and Dr Richardson (who had become his close friend) were planning their next expedition, Eleanor gave birth to a baby girl. John was delighted, and loved playing with the child. One of John's friends said that she looked so much like her father that it was like "looking at Franklin through the wrong end of a telescope". But Eleanor was very ill after the birth, and her health was beginning to give John cause for concern.

We now know that she was suffering from tuberculosis, a serious illness then called "consumption". Today it can usually be treated successfully with antibiotics, but in John and Eleanor's day it was a much feared, unpleasant illness for which there was no cure.

One day, while John was away preparing his ships for the new expedition, a friend stopped by to visit Eleanor. Although Eleanor was full of enthusiasm about the expedition – she proudly displayed a special silk Union Jack that she had made for John to plant in the Arctic – her friend was shocked by her pale and sickly appearance. "I saw, what at that time her own sister had not suspected, that she was dying," she wrote.

Eleanor became seriously ill just before John was due to leave England. He sat with her through the night, praying and reading to her by candlelight from the Bible.

It upset him deeply to witness the suffering she had to endure. At one stage it seemed she would not live to see the next morning – but to everyone's surprise and delight she came through the episode, and, although still very ill, recovered some of her strength.

Knowing how much the expedition meant to her husband, she insisted that John went ahead with it.

***

John and Dr Richardson had learned many lessons from the last trip: instead of relying on vague promises that food would be supplied for them, they sent out as much of their own supplies as possible in advance, and hired an agent in the region to take care of things for them. Lightweight boats were specially built in England and also sent out ahead of the party.

For this expedition, more British seamen and marines were employed, it being John's view that their discipline and willingness to obey orders – vital in harsh and dangerous conditions – could be relied upon to a far greater extent than had been the case with the local helpers hired for the previous trip.

The careful planning paid off for John. This time, despite the inevitable hardships that go hand-in-hand with exploration in such a wild and remote place, there were no disasters or loss of life.

One evening while he was away, John sat down by the shores of a lake to write one of his many letters to Eleanor:

I daily remember you and our little one in our prayers, and I have no doubt that yours are offered up on our behalf... With what heartfelt pleasure I shall embrace you on our return! Your flag is yet snug in the box, and will not be displayed till we get to a more northerly region. Mr Back and the men have arrived ...

He was interrupted by George Back – the officer who had found the Indians on their last expedition and saved the day – touching him lightly on the shoulder.

"There's something I think you should see."

John turned and saw that Back was clutching a newspaper from England "Very well. Leave it beside me, George – I'm just writing to…"

"*John*…"

There was something in Back's voice, a fearful look in his eyes. John guessed immediately what it meant, yet hoped that he might be wrong. He took the newspaper, and it shook slightly in his hand as he read it. After just a few seconds he put it down and picked up the letter again, gazing at it blankly.

There was no one to send it to now. Eleanor, to whom he had been writing almost daily, had lost her struggle for life, and had died eight weeks ago. John felt the loss of his dear wife more keenly than any of the troubles or hardships that he had endured in his life thus far.

During the weeks to come, John kept largely to himself. He carried out his duties as leader of the expedition, but did not join in with the games, dances and lectures with his comrades, as they whiled away the winter months before the weather allowed them to set off again.

There was something he had to do, and the waiting was painful for him. At last, when his expedition reached the coast, John made an excuse while his men were celebrating their arrival, and slipped away. In a still, remote place he planted Eleanor's silk flag in the snow, and whispered a quiet prayer as he gazed out across the ice-strewn Arctic waters.

***

This expedition was a resounding success: it added both to contemporary knowledge of the Arctic coast, and to John's renown as an intrepid explorer. He and his men had ventured into a wilderness that no white man had ever set foot in before, helped to fill in more blank areas on maps, and provided yet more valuable information about the conditions along the coast where a North West Passage might be found.

It was to be John's last voyage of discovery for many years. On November 5th 1828, almost four years after Eleanor's death, he married again, this time to a woman called Jane Griffin.

Jane was a Londoner, and had known Eleanor

before her marriage to John. Indeed she had helped to console John after the death of his wife. Where Eleanor had been artistic and imaginative, Jane was practical and determined – qualities which would be of great value to John in the times ahead.

Two years after his marriage, John was given command of a frigate called the *Rainbow* and was sent to the Mediterranean to help Greece in her struggle to gain independence from Turkey. He was good at calming tempers and getting people to see reason, and as usual he was highly praised for the job he did there.

There had been rumours, while he was away, of a new trip to the Arctic, and once John was back in England Jane encouraged him to put his name forward for the role of leader.

John would have been a very good choice, but in the end the Admiralty went for George Back, the young midshipman who had accompanied John on his first Arctic – now a captain himself.

The job offer that did come John's way was something very different. The government wanted him to be the governor of Van Dieman's Land (now called Tasmania). This island off Australia was controlled by the British, who had started a settlement there some years previously. It was not unusual for senior naval or army officers to be given such posts, but John was worried that it might mean the end of his career as an explorer or sea captain. When the Admiralty assured him that it would not, and, given there were currently no other opportunities available to him, he decided to accept.

John was by now a distinguished man thanks to his fame and achievements. He had been knighted, and was now Sir John Franklin – but this did not impress the senior officials already serving in Van Dieman's Land.

For many people, governing posts in far-flung British colonies like this were simply a means of making lots of money, before they returned home to enjoy their retirement. They did not care about the place itself or the welfare of the inhabitants. but John was an open, honest man who could not undertake any task cynically or lightly.

He hated unfairness and bad practice, and after a brief settling in period as the new governor of Van Dieman's Land, he set about trying to make a number of changes. With the help of Jane he began to establish schools and museums; he also tried to introduce a fairer system for settling disputes. In the past, governors would simply have taken the side of whichever important and influential members of the community was involved. John, though, kept an open mind, and tried to make judgements based on the facts of a case.

This approach went down well with the "ordinary" people of Van Dieman's Land – but not with some of those officials with whom he had to work. In many ways, John, having spent his whole life in the Royal Navy, was unprepared for this world of politics and intrigue. He was shocked and dismayed by the way people were prepared to lie and spread false stories, and he was eventually outplayed by ruthless people who knew the rules of the game much better than him. After seven years, he was recalled to Britain, hurt and embarrassed.

Fortunately for him, the ending of his governorship of Van Dieman's Land could not have come at a better time. Another expedition was in the offing.

Many people now doubted whether it was possible for a ship to forge through the barrier of ice to establish a North West Passage, but the Admiralty had decided to give it one more try.

They were looking for someone to take command of two specially prepared ships, and, now that he was back in England, Captain Sir John Franklin seemed the ideal man for the job. He became one of a very small number of experienced men to make the Admiralty's shortlist.

Chapter Six

It was the spring of 1845, and Queen Victoria was in the early years of her long reign. Photography was a recent invention, miles of railway track was being laid and countless stations were springing up all over the country to serve the new steam trains.

A large crowd of cheering people lined the banks of the river Thames to watch two ships, the *Erebus* and the *Terror,* heavily laden and low in the water, being towed towards the sea. The grinning captain of the *Erebus* took out his handkerchief and waved, having spotted his wife and daughter among the throng. He could not tell whether they had seen him, and he was not to know that this was the last

time he would ever see their faces

The captain was, of course, John Franklin. Internationally known and respected, he was no longer the cherubic, curly haired boy who had anxiously waited to board the *Polyphemus*. In the one and only photograph of him, taken shortly before he was due to lead his North West Passage Expedition, he is seen as a heavily built, balding man. He was now aged fifty-nine.

He was well liked and respected by all who sailed with him, and had for many years been a committed Christian. On this expedition he would lead prayers and worship on his ship every day.

John's two ships would be making use of engines taken from steam trains to power propellers. This was still a new idea. The earliest steam engines drove paddles on the sides of the ship, and the Admiralty had decided to

stage a contest between a paddle-steamer and the *Rattler*, a propeller-driven ship which would be acting as a supply ship for the first stage of John's new expedition.

The two ships performed a tug-of-war on the Thames, connected back-to-back by a strong cable. The *Rattler* won easily, and over the coming years propellers would be added to more and more navy ships and the age of sail would come to an end.

The steam engines would have to be used sparingly on John's ships, however, because of the shortage of room on board for storing the coal that made them work.

For its day, this was a modern, hi-tech expedition. Not only had steam-powered propellers been used but stored below was a vast amount of food kept in sealed tins: another fairly recent invention which would make the food last longer. The two ships themselves had been specially strengthened to protect them against the ice.

It was almost certain that the explorers' task could not be achieved in one summer season: they would not be able to make it from the east side of northern Canada to the west – that is, from the Atlantic Ocean to the Pacific – without having to spend at least one winter stuck in the ice. So they had to be sure they had enough supplies to last them out. They had calculated that they had enough food on both ships to last them for three years. Extra space was also found on board for many hundreds of books to keep the men occupied

This was a very proud moment for John. He wrote to his wife's father shortly before sailing:

I wish you could see this ship now – she is almost as clean as she will be at sea, and quite ready for sailing. The officers and crew all fine young men and in excellent spirits.

And, to his wife, he wrote (the 'Eleanor' mentioned in the letter following is his daughter by his first wife – the little girl had been named after her mother; while 'Sophy' is his niece):

Let me now assure you, my dearest Jane, that I am now amply provided with every requisite for my voyage and that I am entering on my voyage comforted with every hope of God's merciful guidance and protection and especially that He will bless and comfort and protect you my dearest love, my very dear Eleanor and dear Sophy – and all my other relatives.

Oh, how I wish I could write to each of them to assure them of the happiness I feel in my officers, my crew and my ship.

Your affectionate husband,
John Franklin

The two ships made stops at northern Scotland and Greenland, from where some crew members were able to write last letters home. Daniel Bryant, a Royal Marines sergeant, wrote:

I am happy to say that Sir John Franklin is a very religious man and has forbidden all drunkenness and swearing and all bad language…

John, in command of the *Erebus*, had both prepared and entertained his fellow officers by telling
them tales of his previous visits to the Arctic. And,
drawing on his experiences as a young man, he had
prepared a system of signals to be used in case the
two ships became separated by ice or bad weather.

Commander Fitzjames, the first officer, leaves us
with a last impression of Sir John Franklin before
the two ships headed across Baffin Bay, through
Lancaster Sound, and into the unknown:

*He is full of life and energy, with good judgement, and a
capital memory — one of the best I know. His conversation
is delightful and most instructive, and of all men he is the
most fitted for the command of an enterprise requiring
sound sense and great perseverance.*

***

Some time later, two whaling ships returning to
Britain reported that they had sighted the *Erebus* and
Terror, and had spoken with Sir John Franklin and

78

his fellow officers. They reported that everyone had been well, and full of optimism for the journey that lay before them. But this was the last time that John and the 128 other members of the expedition were seen alive by their fellow countrymen.

No one knows exactly what happened to the members of the expedition, and their disappearance remains to this day one of the biggest mysteries of exploration. As the years passed by, and still no word was heard from them, numerous rescue missions were launched — but it was not easy. The region into which John had taken his ships was vast, many times bigger than Great Britain, and was a maze of islands, channels and inlets. Some routes turned out to be dead-ends, others were temporarily blocked by ice. John had had instructions from the Admiralty concerning a couple of possible directions to take, but it was always understood that the further he got into uncharted territory, the more he might have to twist and turn in different directions to avoid a barrier of ice.

On one occasion, John's great friend from his

first Arctic expedition, Dr John Richardson, undertook the gruelling overland trip to the Arctic coast in search of his friend – even though he was around 60 years of age like John. But, like all the other searchers, he found no trace.

Jane continued to pester the Admiralty whenever she felt they weren't doing enough to find her husband, and as time went by people from all over the country wrote to them with suggestions on how he might be found. One man claimed to have been contacted by a ghost who had told him of John's location and that he was alive and well.

Others came up with weird and wonderful ideas for the best methods of searching: but none of them had ever been to the Arctic, and their letters demonstrated that they had no idea what the conditions were like there, or how big the search area was. One man advocated send up an "aeronaut" in a balloon attached to a very long rope so that he could see great distances; another suggested attaching a whole ship to three massive balloons that would lift it above the ice! A sea captain suggested that searchers on bicycles might slither along the ice much quicker than people on foot; and a man wrote from Germany with his designs for an Ice Blowing Up Machine...

Although several ships were sent out by the Admiralty, Jane also spent much of her own money on private expeditions. Finally, five years after John had sailed, the first signs of his last North West Passage Expedition were found on a barren island: pieces of clothing, empty food tins and other items showing that the crews had left their ships and spent time here.

On a neighbouring island the graves of three seamen were discovered. But there was no written record to say what had happened to the rest of the men or where they had been heading for.

***

Years later, in 1854, a Dr Rae, an expert on the Arctic who had earlier accompanied John Richardson in a search, met up with Eskimos, some local people, who told him stories of a group of white men that had starved to death some years earlier. He eventually managed to buy from them items which had obviously belonged to John's expedition: telescopes, watches, cutlery and so on. Some items bore John's own initials. Worse, though, he was shown many bones – bones which bore marks caused by the flesh being cut away. He had no doubt that the starving sailors had resorted to cannibalism – surviving by eating the flesh of their dead comrades – and sent his report back to England.

His findings caused a great stir in the newspapers. Many refused to believe that the sailors had resorted to cannibalism, and instead came to the view that the Eskimos had obtained the white men's belongings after attacking and killing them.

It is an argument that still goes on. The bones

have been analysed in modern times and although tests seem to prove that cannibalism took place, nobody knows how the people died or whether the cannibalism was carried out by Eskimos or the sailors themselves.

British sailors in a tiny number of instances are known to have resorted to saving themselves from starving to death by eating the flesh of their dead – yet it is true that the practice was probably more common among the Eskimos, who were sometimes forced to resort to desperate methods to stay alive in their harsh and unforgiving environment.

Most Eskimos whom the early white explorers encountered were peaceful and friendly, and stories have been passed down to the present day of their people offering starving explorers every assistance. But there were other stories at that time of Eskimo attacks on white men. Indeed, on his second over-land expedition John himself had reported having been attacked by an Eskimo group, intent on killing him and his men for their guns, knives and other useful items.

Some believe that the members of the expedition were poisoned by their own tinned food; it is claimed that the tins then were not made or sealed properly. This may have played some part in the failure of the expedition, but it probably was not the sole cause. A more likely cause was the amount of lead used in sealing the tins in those days – which was often high enough to have caused lead poisoning.

Explorers often built large piles of stones, called cairns, to direct those following after them to messages or food deposits. And in 1859, some five years after Dr Rae's discovery of the bones, such a cairn was found. When the stones were disturbed a sealed container fell out. It contained the only messages from the expedition ever recovered.

There were two notes, both written by some of John's senior officers. The first said that they had spent their first winter on an island (the island where the three graves were later found), and said "All Well". But it seemed that, a couple of years after that note was written, two different officers had returned to the cairn to add a different story. Their note said: "25th April 1848. HM Ships *Terror* and *Erebus* were deserted on the 22nd April, 5 leagues NNW of this having been beset since 12th Sept 1846…" It reported that so far nine officers and 15 men had died, and that the rest were setting off on foot to try and reach the mainland – the very region where John had almost died many years before.

The most significant part of the note concerned John himself: "Sir John Franklin died on the 11th June 1847…"

For some reason, the writer did not give the cause of John's death or any other details. But at least, at long last, 14 years after waving him off from England, Jane knew the truth about her husband. He had succumbed, presumably to some illness, only two years after setting sail.

After this confirmation of his death, Jane pressed for John Franklin to be recognised as the discoverer of the North West Passage, since the various expeditions under his command had "put a roof on the map of Canada", as one writer put it. But in fact no one would manage to sail through from one side of the Arctic to the other in one voyage until Roald Amundsen, the man who was to later to beat Captain Scott to the South Pole, finally sailed from east to west between 1903-1907 .

Most books on the subject do credit Sir John Franklin as the 'discoverer of the North West Passage'. For, although he never managed to sail all the way through it, the expeditions under his command, when taken as a whole, were found to have covered just about all of the Passage.

Let us hope that the former little boy from Spilsby who wanted more than anything else to sail away and explore unknown lands, realised his achievement before he died. Perhaps this knowledge comforted him in his last hours, before he was finally laid to rest in the icy wilderness to which he had always been drawn.

Quiz

After you've finished the book, test yourself and see how well you remember what you've read.

1. The traditional hairstyle for a sailor in the late 18th century was:
A crewcut
A long plait
A mullet

2. On board ship, 'a nipper' was:
A boy who helped pull up the anchor
A type of insect that bit people in their sleep
A particularly cold wind from the east

3. What was the Navy's signal to begin battle?
Thunderbirds Are Go
Action Stations
Clear for Action

4. How long did it take John Franklin's relative Capt Flinders to sail from England to Australia?
10 days
10 weeks
10 months

5. The recommended cure for scurvy was:
Eating plenty of fresh fruit and vegetables
Washing in fresh urine daily
Drinking two litres of fresh water a day

6.On seeing French warships while on their way back from China, the British merchant navy decided to:
Pretend they were battleships and attack
Hide in port until the danger passed
Surrender

7.Ordinary sailors' nickname for the famous ship the Bellerophon was:
Barrel of Fun
Ballet for One
Billy Ruffian

8.Eleanor Porden came to John Franklin's notice by:
Waving a home-made flag on the dock
Writing a poem about his adventures
Winning a Blue Peter competition to meet your hero

9.During their second visit to the Arctic, the explorers survived on a diet consisting mostly of:
Weeds
Ice cream
Take aways

10.On returning to their camp Fort Enterprise, the explorers discovered that:
The cupboard was bare
The Eskimos had arranged a surprise birthday party for John
Royal Mail had left a card saying they were unable to deliver a hamper from Harrods

11.When the book about the Arctic expedition was published it was:
An immediate bestseller
The inspiration for a long-running soap opera
Turned into a popular board game called 'Frozen North'

12.The beautiful daughter of the explorers' Eskimo interpreter was called:
Greensleeves
Green Goddess
Greenstockings

13.What did his wife Eleanor make for John Franklin to take on his second trip to the Arctic?
A silk Union Jack
Her special protein-rich carrot cake
A set of knitted underwear

14.The island of Tasmania used to be known as:
Van Helsing's Territory
Van Morrison's Backyard
Van Dieman's Land

15.In 1845 John Franklin was:
49 years old
59 years old
69 years old

16.For Franklin's third expedition, the Admiralty provided him with:
Ships with steam-powered propellers

Solar-powered hovercraft

Diesel-powered snowmobiles

17.As Captain of the Erebus, Franklin banned sailors from:

Swearing

Farting

Nose-picking

18.Ideas on how to look for Franklin's the missing third expedition included:

Sending off a search party on bicycles

Fitting miniature cameras to Arctic eagles

Asking the advice of every fortune-teller in the country

19.Dr Rae's report of his discovery of human remains claimed that:

The sailors had resorted to cannibalism

They had been murdered by Eskimos

They had died from food poisoning

20.After his death, John Franklin was hailed as the man who:

Put a roof on Canada

Made a tunnel through the Arctic

Built a bridge across the top of the world

KEY DATES

1786 – Born in Spilsby, Lincolnshire, 16 April

1800 – Joined HMS *Polyphemus*

1801 – Battle of Copenhagen; joined HMS *Investigator*

1803 – Shipwrecked on *Porpoise*

1804 – Battle with French squadron on *Earl Camden*; joined HMS *Bellerophon*

1805 – Battle of Trafalgar

1807 – Joined HMS *Bedford*

1808 – Promoted to lieutenant

1815 – Took part in attack on New Orleans during war with USA

1818 – North Pole expedition in command of HMS *Trent*

1819 – Left England on first overland expedition to Canada Promoted to commander

1822 – Promoted to captain

1823 – Married Eleanor Anne Porden

1825 – Second overland expedition to Canada. Death of Eleanor

1828 – Married Jane Griffin

1829 – Received knighthood

1830 – Joined HMS *Rainbow* stationed in Mediterranean

1836 – Sailed to Van Dieman's Land (Tasmania) to become Lieutenant Governor

1845 – Sailed on HMS *Erebus* in search of North West Passage

1847 – Died in Arctic, 11 June

Author biography

Martyn Beardsley is the author of six "Sir Gadabout"
books for Orion's Dolphin series. He also recently
published *The Bell Tower* (Harcourt Educational). He lives
in Beeston, near Nottingham, and is married with
one daughter.

Dear Reader,

No matter how old you are, good books always leave you wanting to know more. If you have any questions you would like to ask the author, **Martyn Beardsley,** about **Sir John Franklin** please write to us at: SHORT BOOKS 15 Highbury Terrace, London N5 1UP.

If you enjoyed this title, then you would probably enjoy others in the series. Why not click on our website for more information and see what the teachers are being told? **www.shortbooks.co.uk**

All the books in the WHO WAS... series are available from TBS, Distribution Centre, Colchester Road, Frating Green, Colchester, Essex CO7 7DW
(Tel: 01206 255800), at £4.99 + P&P.